STEP-UP
SCIENCE

Circuits
and Conductors

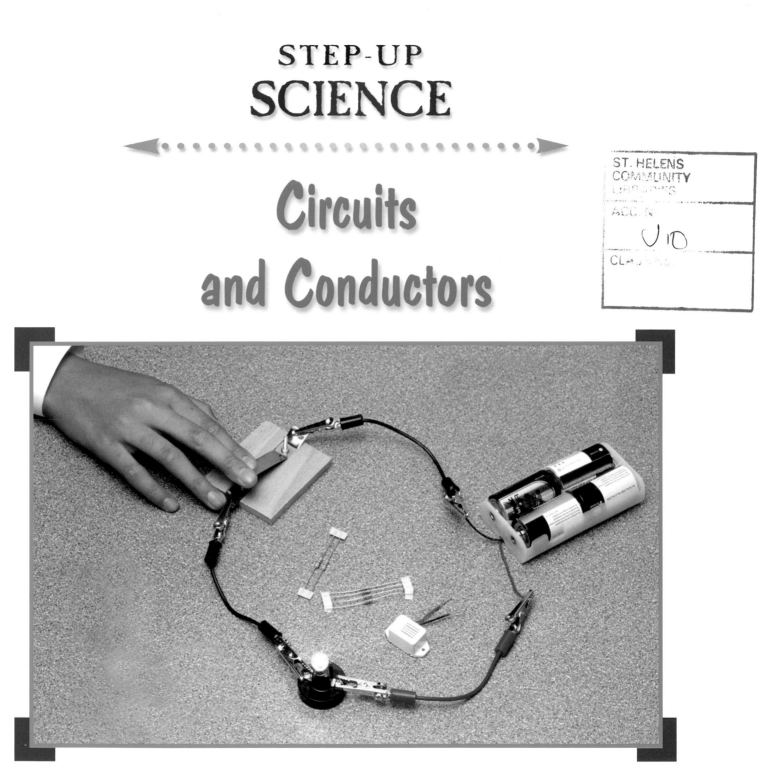

Louise and Richard Spilsbury

Evans

Published by Evans Brothers Limited
2A Portman Mansions
Chiltern Street
London W1U 6NR

Reprinted 2009

Produced for Evans Brothers Limited by
White-Thomson Publishing Ltd,
Bridgewater Business Centre,
210 High Street,
Lewes, East Sussex BN7 2NH

Printed in China by New Era Printing Co. Ltd

Project manager: Harriet Brown

Designer: Flick, Book Design and Graphics

Consultant: Jackie Holderness,
educational consultant and writer

British Library Cataloguing in Publication Data

Circuits and Conductors – (Step-up Science)

1. Electric circuits – Juvenile literature

2. Electric conductivity – Juvenile literature

621.3'192

ISBN: 9780237532123

Acknowledgements:

The authors would like to thank Scott Fisher,
teacher at Stokenham Area Primary School for his
invaluable comments and advice on this series.

Picture acknowledgements:

Martyn f. Chillmaid: cover (top right), pages 1, 4, 6,
7 (all), 8, 9bl, 10c, 11 (all), 13bl, 14 (all), 15, 16,
19, 23l, 27, 29b. CORBIS: cover (main) (Roger
Ressmeyer), 5br (Royalty Free), 16-17 (Roger
Ressmeyer). Ecoscene: pages 23r, 24, 25tr.
Istockphoto: cover (top left), 5tl, 9tr, 9br, 10l, 10r,
12t, 17r, 18 (all), 21, 26, 28, 29t. Oxford Scientific:
page 22 (Imagestate Ltd. Photographer: Surbey
Charlie). Science Photo Library: page 25bl (Ted
Kinsman).

Illustrations by Ian Thompson (pages 13t and 20).

Contents

What is electricity?

Many of us use computers, lights and televisions each day without really thinking about what makes them work. These machines are powered by electricity. Electricity is a type of energy. The electricity we use comes from two sources: mains electricity and batteries.

Mains electricity

Mains electricity comes from power stations. These are factories that create electricity using a generator. Electricity travels from the power station through cables to our homes (see pages 20–21). Machines that use mains electricity only work when they are plugged into a wall socket and switched on. Mains electricity is powerful and can be very dangerous (see pages 26–27).

▲ Look at this image. How many appliances can you see that are powered by electricity?

Life in the past

Can you imagine what life was like before people had mains electricity available in their homes? Look at the image above. How do you think the jobs done by these appliances were done in the past? Write a description for each job.

Batteries

Batteries produce smaller amounts of electricity than mains electricity. They usually last for a short time but are useful for providing power for portable devices such as mp3 players and mobile phones. Some batteries are disposable, which means that we throw them away when

What is a circuit?

Electrical circuits are loops or pathways along which electricity can flow. An electrical circuit always requires a supply of electricity. When we plug an appliance like a lamp into a mains socket in a wall and switch it on, electricity starts to flow into the cable. It flows through the cable to the lamp to make it work, and then returns through the cable to the socket in one unbroken loop. Electricity will only flow if the circuit is complete.

▲ *These appliances are all battery-powered. Try to name three more battery-powered appliances that you find in the home.*

they run out. Other batteries can be recharged to full power again. Why do you think toys that run on electricity are often battery-powered?

Although batteries do not usually supply massive amounts of electricity, it is important never to open a battery. They are full of dangerous chemicals.

▲ *The electrical energy stored in the batteries of these games consoles only provide power when they are connected properly in a circuit.*

Making circuits

We can make a simple electrical circuit using just three components (parts). Firstly, we need a source of electricity, such as a battery. Secondly, we need a device to be powered by the electricity, such as a light bulb or a motor. Finally, we need wires to connect the other components together to make a circuit and allow the electricity to flow.

An electrical circuit

To make any device work using electricity, you need a complete circuit. For the circuit shown on the right, the electricity must be able to flow from the battery to the bulb, and back to the battery, without a break in the circuit. The bulb lights up when electricity flows through it. Why do the wires need to be connected securely?

Connecting a battery

Every battery has two terminals. One is positive and is marked +. One is negative and is marked –. Electricity always flows from the negative terminal of a battery. It can only return to the positive terminal after flowing through an unbroken circuit.

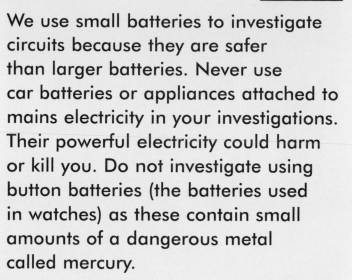

Be safe!

We use small batteries to investigate circuits because they are safer than larger batteries. Never use car batteries or appliances attached to mains electricity in your investigations. Their powerful electricity could harm or kill you. Do not investigate using button batteries (the batteries used in watches) as these contain small amounts of a dangerous metal called mercury.

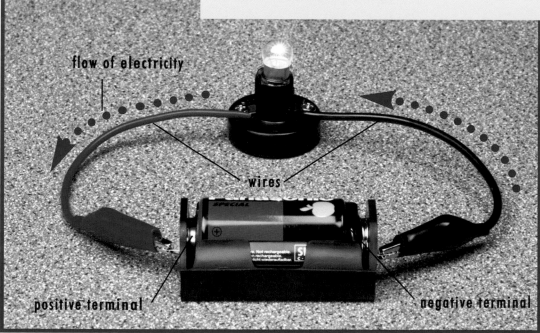

flow of electricity

wires

positive terminal

negative terminal

▲ Electricity is travelling out of the right-hand side of the battery (the negative terminal), to the bulb, and back to the left-hand side of the battery (the positive terminal).

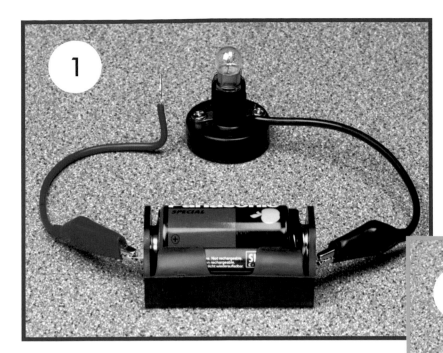

Take a closer look

These three circuits have been set up in the classroom. Can you explain whether any of them will work and light the bulb? If they will not work, try to explain why. How would you fix them and complete the circuits?

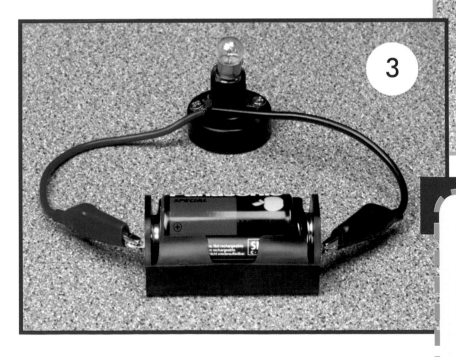

See for yourself

If you have the necessary equipment – two wires with crocodile clips on their ends, a battery and small light bulb – connect them together to make a simple circuit. If you do not have the equipment, draw and label a circuit using the same components. Label the positive and negative terminals of the battery. Which way will the electricity flow?

Batteries and bulbs

Batteries come in different shapes and sizes, and each one has a different power capability. A battery does not contain electricity. Instead, it contains chemicals that react together and produce electricity. When the battery is connected in a circuit, it pushes the electricity around the circuit. We measure the push in units called volts (V). The pushing power of a battery is its voltage.

Battery power

Bulbs and motors are designed for use with a particular voltage. For example, if you have a torch that holds a 1.5V bulb, it needs to run on a 1.5V battery. If a battery is not powerful enough for a device, then the device will not work properly. If a battery is too powerful, then the electricity could damage the device.

Using two or more batteries

Some devices run on two or more batteries. This increases the amount of power they receive. If you use more than one battery, you must make sure that all the batteries are facing the correct way. The positive terminal of one battery should connect to the negative terminal of the next, otherwise the electricity will not flow.

Alessandro Volta

Italian doctor Alessandro Volta invented the first battery in 1800. Look up his name on the Internet and find out how he came up with the idea for a battery while dissecting a frog. Describe what the first battery looked like. Did it look anything like modern batteries?

Light bulbs

If you look at a light bulb you can see two wires connected by a curly wire called a filament. These wires form part of the circuit. As electricity flows through the filament, it becomes hotter and hotter, until it glows white hot and gives off light. When we say a bulb has 'blown', it means that the filament has broken in two.

The filament in a light bulb looks short but it is actually ▶ a very long, thin wire coiled up like a spring. Look at a real light bulb with a magnifying glass to see the filament. Do not touch a light bulb that is switched on or has only recently been switched off – it will be hot.

filament

The small cylindrical batteries shown on page 8 are 1.5V batteries. Larger 1.5V batteries last longer than smaller 1.5V batteries. The upright rectangular battery (left) is a 9V battery. The large car battery (right) is a 12V battery. With an adult's help, look at some batteries at home. You will see the voltage written on them.

Switching on and off

Think about how many switches we use every day. We switch on and off lights, computers, radios, CD players, kettles and toasters. Take a look around the room that you are in and count how many appliances use switches.

How switches work

We know that electrical circuits must have a complete path so that electricity can flow. If a circuit is incomplete, the electricity cannot flow. A switch makes or breaks a circuit.

A switch opens a gap in the circuit so that electricity cannot flow to the appliance. This is what happens when you turn off a switch. When you turn it on again, the gap in the circuit closes to make the circuit complete, and the electricity flows to the appliance.

Why do we need switches?

Switches make electrical appliances useful and safe. Switches help us save electricity. When the circuit is broken, the appliance stops using up electricity.

▲ Switches are useful because they give you control over an electrical circuit.

▼ When you push a button on a remote control, you are completing a circuit.

If we did not have a switch to turn off a light, we would have to remove the bulb. Switches allow appliances to last longer. If a machine worked continuously, its parts would soon become worn out or damaged.

Investigating switches

To make a simple switch, we can use a paper clip that connects two wires to complete a circuit (on), and separates the wires to break the circuit (off).

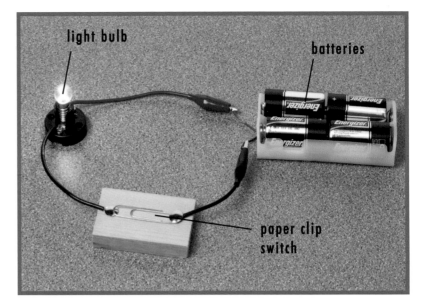

light bulb

batteries

paper clip switch

▲ *This circuit uses a paper clip as a switch. What would you need to do to switch the light off?*

Spring-loaded switches

When you push a **doorbell**, you complete a circuit and a buzzer makes a sound. The doorbell is a spring-loaded switch. When you take your finger off it, a spring pushes the ends of the circuit apart and breaks the circuit. The buzzer stops. The photograph below shows a home-made spring-loaded switch.

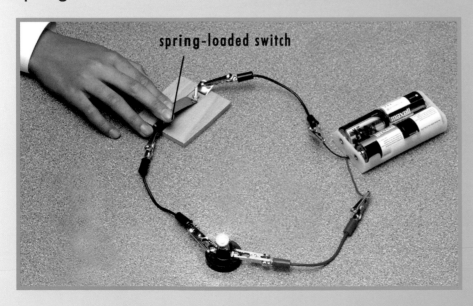

spring-loaded switch

Make a funfair game

At a fair you may have tested how steady your hand is by moving a loop along a twisty wire. When the wires touch, a buzzer sounds because you have completed a circuit. These online instructions will help you make your own game: http://www.worsleyschool.net/science/files/steady/hand.html

Circuit symbols

We can use words or pictures to describe how a circuit is connected together. We can also use electrical symbols to draw a circuit diagram.

Electrical symbols are drawn in the same way all over the world. They allow people from different countries to understand and interpret circuits. Drawing circuits with symbols is a very clear way to communicate.

▲ *Circuit diagrams provide instructions to people who build houses or machines. The diagram tells them where to put the electrical components.*

Using circuit symbols

A circuit diagram includes the components of a circuit and shows how they are connected. It is similar to making a map of a circuit.

Looking at circuit symbols

These are the most commonly used circuit symbols.

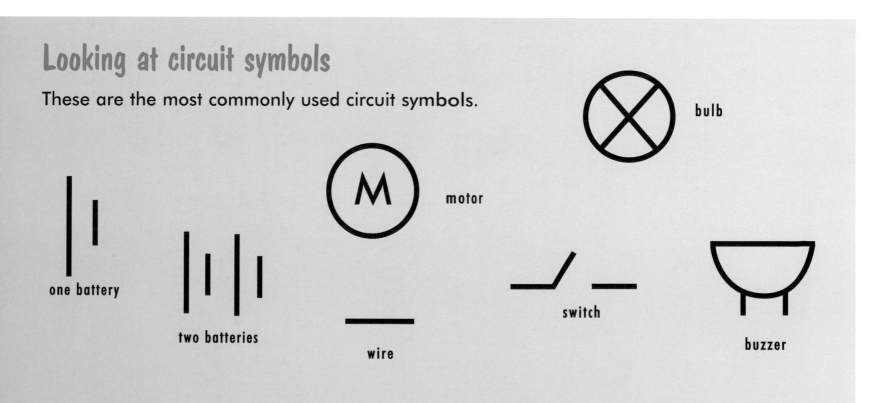

one battery

two batteries

motor

wire

switch

bulb

buzzer

A torch circuit is fairly simple. The negative terminal at the end of the batteries is connected to the switch. The switch is connected to a light bulb, and the light bulb is connected to the positive terminal at the other end of the set of batteries to complete the circuit. Why do all of the batteries have to point in the same direction?

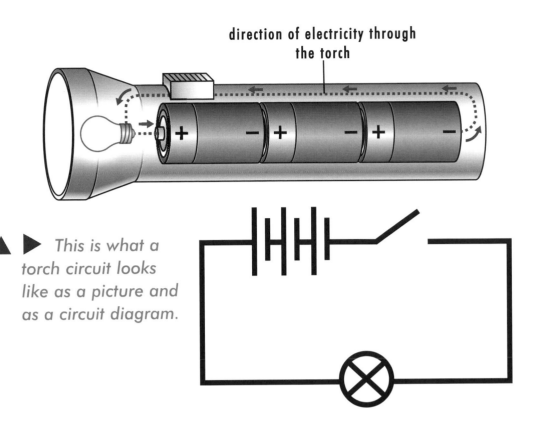

direction of electricity through the torch

▲ ▶ *This is what a torch circuit looks like as a picture and as a circuit diagram.*

Looking at a circuit diagram

Two switches can operate one buzzer. For example, some houses have a doorbell switch on the garage door and one on the front door. Both switches can be connected to one buzzer in one circuit, as shown in the circuit diagram on the right. Can you explain how this works by interpreting the circuit diagram?

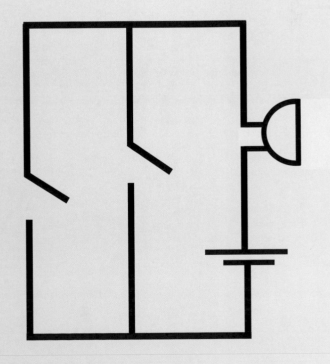

Investigating circuits

You can change a circuit by adding more powerful batteries, different appliances, another loop of wire or thicker or thinner wire. For example, extra battery power will make a light bulb glow more brightly. If there are many bulbs in a circuit, they will all be dimmer than if there were only one bulb.

One or more bulbs

In a simple circuit that contains wire, one battery and one light bulb, the bulb will glow when the circuit is connected correctly. What do you think will happen if a second light bulb is connected in the circuit?

Both light bulbs glow because the electricity is flowing through the complete circuit. The flow of electricity from the battery is constant no matter how many bulbs are in the circuit. However, the more bulbs there are in the circuit, the dimmer each one will be.

More power

When the voltage of a battery in a circuit is increased, the electricity is pushed harder. This means that it flows faster and does more work. How could you increase the voltage in a circuit? How would this change the brightness of the bulb in the circuit?

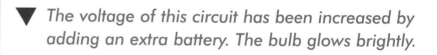

▼ *The voltage of this circuit has been increased by adding an extra battery. The bulb glows brightly.*

▲ *These bulbs are dimly lit because they are connected to only one battery.*

Thick or thin wires

What happens if we change the thickness of the wires in a circuit? Electricity flows faster through thick wires than through thin ones because there is more space.

A hose pipe is like a wire. The water travelling through it is like electricity. If you squeeze the hose, the water cannot travel through as quickly. You are causing resistance. In the same way, a thin wire causes resistance in an electrical circuit. Plan an experiment to test resistance in a circuit. How do you think the length of the wire would affect resistance?

▲ When a hose pipe is squeezed, the water cannot flow through as freely. There is more resistance. The same is true in an electrical circuit. A thin wire provides more resistance than a thick wire.

Measuring brightness

Hold a sheet of white paper in front of a glowing bulb and you can see the light shining through. Do you think you would see more or less light with two sheets?

You can use this method to compare the brightness of two or more light bulbs.

Light bulbs

Predict how many identical light bulbs will work with just one battery. Plan a fair test to investigate this. How will you measure the brightness? If you have the equipment at home or at school, you could carry out the test to see if your prediction was correct. You could present your results to your classmates.

Electrical conductors

Metal wires are used in electrical circuits because metal is a good conductor. An electrical conductor is a material that allows electricity to flow through it easily. Some types of material conduct electricity more easily than others.

Which materials are conductors?

Conductors are usually metals, such as iron, copper and lead, but metals do not all conduct electricity with equal efficiency. Many forms of carbon are good electrical conductors too, such as graphite, from which some pencil leads are made. Although water is a poor conductor compared to metal, it can still conduct electricity.

Lightning conductors

Lightning is a form of electricity. When tiny pieces of ice inside clouds rub against each other again and again, electricity builds up in the clouds. This friction can create sparks that jump suddenly towards the Earth as a flash of lightning. A lightning bolt is incredibly hot and can set buildings on fire. Some tall buildings have lightning conductor rods on top of them. These metal rods conduct the electricity safely into the ground.

WARNING

Always dry your hands before you touch anything electrical. Water can work its way into the device and conduct electricity to your body. Electric shocks can badly burn or kill you.

Using electrical conductors

Copper is one of the best metal conductors and aluminium is one of the worst. Therefore, copper is often used in mains electricity cables and to make the prongs on a plug. When you push a plug into a socket it conducts electricity from the socket through the plug and up through the wires into a device, such as a toaster or radio.

▲ Lightning bolts find the quickest way to the ground. When tall buildings are nearby, the quickest route can be through a building.

▲ You can see the copper wires coming out of this cable. Copper conducts electricity quickly from place to place.

Make a circuit detector

Brass is a good conductor of electricity. Have fun making a secret circuit using brass paper fasteners. Ask an adult to help you make a circuit detector to work out where a wire is hidden. Go to the following website:

http://www.chemistry.org/portal/ a/c/s/1/educatorsandstudents.html When you get there, click on the following links to find the circuit detector project: 'WonderNet', 'View all topics' and lastly 'Electric circuits'.

Electrical insulators

Metals are good conductors of electricity but most other materials are not. Materials that do not conduct electricity well are called insulators. Electrical insulators are the opposite of electrical conductors.

Insulators

Electrical insulators include glass, cloth, rubber and plastic. If you put an insulating material in a circuit, it can stop the flow of electricity. Insulators can be useful when we want to stop electricity flowing. Metal wires are usually covered in plastic because the plastic insulator makes sure the electricity only travels along the wire. If a wire was not insulated, the electricity would flow along any conductor that came into contact with the wire, including humans.

Insulating appliances

Many electrical appliances are covered in materials that are good electrical insulators. The insulating materials prevent people from receiving an electric shock from the metal wires inside. Plugs and wall sockets are made of rubber or plastic for the same reason. Think about other electrical appliances that we use at home, such as an electric toothbrush. Plastic is used to protect our fingers from touching the metal parts.

▲ The glass disks in this picture help prevent the electricity that runs through the power lines from travelling down the pole to the ground, where it could give people a shock.

▲ A plug's cover is made of rubber or plastic because these materials are good insulators.

Investigating conductors and insulators

Make a circuit like the one below. Test the conductivity of different materials by connecting them in the circuit. Test at least six materials in your investigation, including a pencil. Predict which materials will complete the circuit properly and light the bulb. What happens when you complete the circuit using the pencil? Why must it be sharpened at each end first? Which of the materials was the best conductor? Record your results in a table.

▲ Which of these objects or materials will complete the circuit and light the bulb?

Test insulators online

You don't need to make a circuit to test which materials make good conductors and insulators. You can visit http://www.bbc.co.uk/schools/scienceclips/ages/8_9/circuits_conductors.shtml to test several different materials.

How electricity gets to our homes

Mains electricity is usually made by generators in a power station. It flows from the power station in a giant circuit to reach our homes and schools. The electricity may have to travel hundreds of kilometres before we use it.

Generating electricity

Fossil fuels such as oil, coal and gas are burnt to heat water and produce steam. The steam moves through pipes into a turbine, which is rather like a paddle wheel. The steam spins the turbine. The turbine turns the generator and this makes electricity.

Some power stations use nuclear power to heat the water instead of burning fossil fuels. Other power stations use more environmentally friendly energy sources, such as wind energy, wave energy and solar energy to produce electricity.

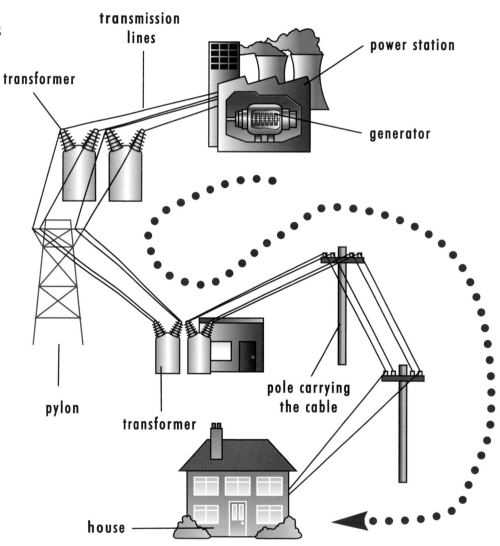

▼ *This diagram shows the route that electricity takes from a power station to your home.*

transmission lines

transformer

power station

generator

pylon

transformer

pole carrying the cable

house

Distributing the power

The electricity produced by a power station flows into a machine called a transformer. The transformer increases the voltage to push the electricity over long distances. The electricity flows through thick cables called transmission lines that stretch across the country, held up by giant metal towers called pylons.

Going home

When the electricity nears homes, schools, factories and other buildings, transformers lower the voltage. This makes the electricity safer to distribute. Before electricity reaches our homes, it often travels in underground cables.

The electricity flows into our homes through an electricity meter, which measures how much electricity is used. From there, it travels through wires to the sockets and switches.

◀ *Pylons hold up the transmission lines which carry electricity hundreds of kilometres to your home.*

Comparing voltages

Torch battery = 1.5V

Mains electricity = 240V

Power station generator = 25,000V

Overhead powerline = 400,000V

Lightning flash = 100 million V

Environmentally friendly fuel

Imagine that your family want to switch from fossil fuel electricity to solar energy electricity. How much might it cost to install solar panels on the roof of your home? Use the Internet to try to find out an approximate cost.

Using electricity

We can use electricity to make many different appliances work. Electrical appliances produce heat, light, sound or movement.

Electricity for heat

Appliances that heat up, such as an electric kettle or toaster, change electrical energy into heat energy. They do this by using a resistor. A resistor slows down the flow of electricity.

When you turn on a toaster, electricity flows from the plug into a heating element. This contains loops of thin wire made of high-resistance metal. The high-resistance metal slows down the electricity flow and some of the electrical energy turns to heat energy. The wires glow red hot and toast your bread.

Electricity for light

High-resistance filaments in light bulbs glow when electricity flows through them. However, energy-efficient light bulbs do not have filaments. They are thin glass tubes that contain gases.

Turn the sound down

A volume knob changes how much sound a CD player produces. A metal pointer inside the switch touches a loop of high-resistance wire. When you turn the knob, the pointer moves along the loop of wire. This changes the distance that the electricity must travel. The further it travels, the greater the resistance and the quieter the sound becomes.

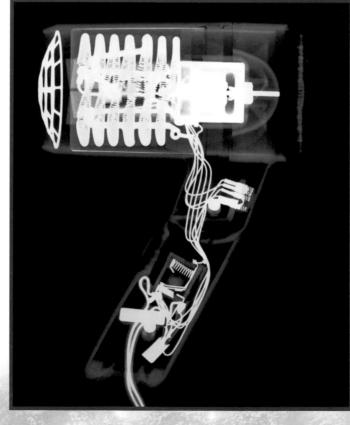

◀ *Hair dryers have high-resistance wires coiled inside them. The wires become hot when electricity flows through them. A motor operates a fan, which blows air across the wires, heating them up.*

The insides of the glass tubes in energy-efficient light bulbs are sprayed with a coating that is similar to glow-in-the-dark paint. When electricity flows through the gases, it makes the coating glow brightly.

Electricity for movement

Many machines have motors. These are appliances that convert electrical energy into movement (kinetic) energy. Motors in washing machines and food processors turn barrels and blades around. Motors in a dishwasher squirt in water to clean plates, while those in a vacuum cleaner create suction that picks up dust from the floor.

▲ Neon lights contain gases. When electricity passes through them, the gases cause the bulbs to glow.

◄ A food mixer contains a motor that turns the mixing blade. The motor is powered by electricity.

Saving energy

Have you ever been told to 'Turn off those lights!' or 'Close the door!' because you are wasting electricity? How does leaving lights on or leaving doors open waste electricity? Why should we save electricity?

Saving money

Electricity meters measure the amount of electricity we use. Every few months, the meter is checked and we pay for the electricity we have used. Using a lot of electricity means large bills for families to pay. Using less electricity saves us money.

Saving resources

Using less electricity also saves the world's natural resources. Most of our electricity is made by burning fossil fuels such as coal, oil and gas. Fossil fuels take many millions of years to form in the ground. One day they will run out, which is why they are called non-renewable resources. Burning fossil fuels also causes air pollution. It puts harmful gases into the air we breathe. The less electricity we use, the less air pollution there will be.

This is a large coal mine in Scotland. Coal is a fossil fuel. Many scientists argue that we should be using alternative energy sources to heat and light our homes, such as wind, wave and solar energy.

Energy efficiency

Learn more about energy-saving electrical devices, such as energy-efficient fridges and light bulbs, on the Internet. These devices are designed to run on very little electricity. Make a poster to persuade people to buy these products instead of appliances that use more electricity.

How to save energy

In winter, warm air from your house can seep outside through gaps around windows and doors and make your home colder. That means your heaters have to work harder to keep you warm. In doing so, they use up more electricity. To solve this problem, people insulate their homes. When we insulate a home, we put layers of insulating material in roofs and walls to prevent heat from escaping. We can also install double-glazed windows. These have two layers of glass that trap a layer of air. The layer of air insulates the room.

▲ The roof of this house is covered with solar panels to collect the Sun's energy and turn it into electricity.

▲ This image shows waste heat escaping from a house. The white areas are the hottest and the blue areas are the coolest.

Make a difference

There are many things you can do every day to save electricity.

1. Open the fridge door as little as possible.

2. Turn off lights, radios, televisions and computers when you are not using them.

3. Keep doors and windows closed when the heating is on.

4. Never leave electrical appliances on standby. One report found that people in the UK waste around two power stations' worth of electricity each year by leaving televisions and other gadgets on standby.

Playing it safe

Mains electricity and some types of battery can harm us. It is vital that we all know how to deal with electricity safely.

 Never stick anything other than a plug in an electrical socket. Never put a metal object into a toaster.

 Never put too many plugs into an adaptor. This can make too much electricity flow through the socket and cause a fire.

 When you unplug an electrical appliance, pull it out by the plug, not by the cord.

 Only fly kites in open spaces, never around power lines. If your kite looks as though it will become tangled in a power line, let go of it immediately. Electricity can travel from the kite to you.

 Never use or touch an electrical appliance that has frayed cables. The insulating layer has been damaged.

Never touch anything electrical with wet hands.

This firefighter is using a powder fire extinguisher. Powder and carbon dioxide fire extinguishers are used to put out electrical fires. If water is used, it could conduct the electricity to the firefighter.

Fuses and safety

Electrical appliances can be damaged and sometimes catch fire if too much electricity flows through them at once. For example, if you add too many batteries to a circuit you will burn out your light bulb. To protect people who use electrical appliances, plugs have fuses. A fuse is a thin, high-resistance wire. If mains electricity suddenly becomes too powerful, for example, when there is lightning, the fuse becomes overloaded

▲ Never put batteries in a fire or cut them open. The chemicals inside are very dangerous.

▲ Always dispose of old batteries safely. There is usually a collection point at a waste disposal site for old batteries.

▲ If someone receives an electric shock from touching an appliance, use a wooden or plastic object to knock the appliance away from the person. Do not touch the person.

and burns out. This breaks the circuit and stops the extra electricity flowing to the appliance. This can prevent a fire. Fuses are also called circuit breakers.

▶ *Why is it important to make sure you have a fuse in a plug?*

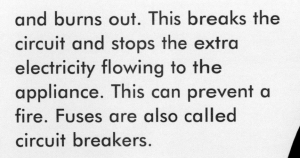

A closer look at a plug

Ask an adult to help you use a screwdriver to take apart a plug that is not attached to a socket or an appliance. Can you find the fuse? Draw a picture to show the coloured wires and how they are arranged. If you take the fuse out, you should be able to see a certain number of amps printed on the side of it. Try to find out what the word amps is short for and what amps measure. Carry out some Internet research to find out the purpose of each of the wires in a plug.

Glossary

air pollution   harmful gases in the air.

amp   short for ampere, the unit we use to measure the electric current.

battery   a container of chemicals that produces electricity when properly connected in a circuit.

circuit   a path or loop along which electricity can travel.

circuit diagram   a scientific drawing that shows all the components of a circuit and how they are joined together.

component   part of an electrical circuit.

conduct   to carry electricity (or heat).

conductor   an object or material that allows heat or electricity to flow through it easily.

electricity   a type of energy we use as a source of power to make machines work.

electric shock   when electricity flows suddenly through a person. Small shocks can hurt slightly; large shocks can kill.

energy   the ability to move or do work.

filament   the part of a bulb that glows when electricity passes through it.

fossil fuels   fuels formed over millions of years by the remains of ancient plants and animals.

friction   a force that resists motion between two objects.

fuse   a thin, high resistance wire that burns out easily to break a circuit.

generator   a machine that produces electricity.

insulator   an object or material that resists or stops the flow of electricity.

lightning   a giant spark of electricity that travels between clouds or from a cloud to Earth.

mains electricity   electricity made in power stations that is delivered to homes and other buildings.

motor   a machine that changes electrical energy into movement energy.

natural resources materials from the Earth, such as water, coal and soil.

non-renewable describes a resource that cannot be replaced once it is used up.

plug a device with two or three prongs that we put into a socket to make an electrical connection.

power station a factory where electricity is made.

resistance how much a material slows or stops the flow of electricity.

resistor a device that slows down the flow of electricity.

socket a place to insert a plug and connect an electrical appliance to an electricity supply.

solar energy the energy from sunlight. Solar energy is used to generate electricity.

switch a device that closes or opens a gap in a circuit to control electricity flow. Switches turn machines on and off.

symbol something used in place of a real picture. Symbols do not always look exactly like the object that they represent.

terminal point on a battery from which electricity can flow or return. A terminal can be positive or negative.

volt a unit that measure voltage.

voltage a force that pushes electricity through a wire.

For teachers and parents

This book is designed to support and extend the learning objectives for Unit 4F of the QCA Science Schemes of Work.

The children may have some experience with making circuits, which this book builds upon. The book also helps the children to understand the relevance and importance of electricity, science and technology in everyday life and recognise risks to themselves to do with electricity.

Throughout this book and throughout their own investigative work children should be aware that science is based on evidence and they should have the opportunity to:

- Turn questions and ideas into investigations.
- Decide which apparatus to use.
- Predict results.
- Understand the need to collect sufficient evidence.
- Understand the need to conduct a fair test.
- Construct circuits and investigate how they work.
- Use ICT and other methods to record results.
- Work out for themselves what their results mean and how to explain them.

There are opportunities for cross-curricular work in history, literacy, numeracy, art, design technology and ICT.

SUGGESTED FURTHER ACTIVITIES

Pages 4 - 5 What is electricity?

To reinforce the idea of electricity flowing in a circuit you could try the following activity, perhaps during a physical education class:

Give a circle of children a ball to pass from hand to hand to each other as quickly as they can. This represents electricity travelling round a circuit. Then ask them to form another shape, but remain in a loop and pass the ball again. This shows the way that it does not matter if we alter the shape of a circuit because the electricity can still flow round it.

Children can find out more about the history of electricity at http://www.digitalbrain.com/digitalbrain/web/subjects/1.%20primary/ks2sci/su4/mod1/exercise1.db_psc?verb=view

Pages 6 - 7 Making circuits

At http://www.crocodile-clips.com you can download free simulation software that allows children to build circuits on-screen using pictorial components, and adding text and images as they go.

At http://www.bbc.co.uk/schools/podsmission/electricity/annie02.shtml the children can help a character called Annie build a circuit online.

Set up some simple circuits with faults for children to mend. For example, the circuit might have a broken bulb, a bulb that is loose in the holder or a wire that is not fastened to the battery.

Pages 8 - 9 Batteries and bulbs

Children could look at the type of metal from which bulb filaments are made and from which they have been made in the past. Tungsten is often used as it can be heated close to its melting point without evaporating rapidly.

Make a lemon battery with instructions from the BBC website: http://www.bbc.co.uk/schools/podsmission/electricity/pod.shtml

The following website is all about batteries, and has good information on the history of batteries: http://www.energizer.com/learning/

Pages 10 - 11 Switching on and off

To explain the idea of a broken circuit, the children could repeat the ball travelling around the circle activity, but then ask one of the children to step out and break the circuit. (The ball cannot be thrown and the children should not be standing too close together.) Electricity (the ball) stops moving or flowing round the circuit when the circuit has a gap in it.

At http://www.digitalbrain.com/document.server/subjects/ks2sci/su4/images/bulbs5.rm children can watch a short video showing them how to make a switch.

Once the children have the idea of making a basic circuit with switches, they could use this knowledge to use a circuit and bulb to make a model lighthouse. Or they could make a simple robot with eyes that light up using the template and instructions at http://www.electricityineducation.co.uk/assets/pdf/KS2%20Worksheet%203.pdf

Pages 12 - 13 Circuit symbols

The children could design and make a matching pairs or snap card game using the circuit symbols to help them learn all of the symbols.

Pages 14 - 15 Investigating circuits

Ask children to predict and investigate what would happen if they put a knot in a circuit wire. More able students could also be asked to make a circuit with a light and a buzzer so that they both work at the same time.

Pages 16 - 17 Circuit conductors

Lightning is static electricity. Children could find out more about static electricity and Benjamin Franklin, who was lucky to survive his experiment of flying a kite in a thunder storm.

They could try making static electricity with a balloon at http://www.digitalbrain.com/digitalbrain/web/subjects/1.%20primary/ks2sci/su4/mod1/exercise2.db_psc?verb=view

Pages 18 - 19 Electrical insulators

There are some excellent sheets to download about insulators and other relevant electricity information for KS2 children for parents and teachers at http://www.hep.phys.soton.ac.uk/hycs/electricity.pdf

Pages 20 - 21 How electricity gets to our homes

Children could investigate how a generator creates electricity from the starting point of a bike dynamo, which converts the movement of a wheel into electricity to power bike lights. A power plant generator moves a huge magnet near a wire to create a steady flow of electricity.

At http://www.brainpop.com/science/energy/currentelectricity/ children can watch a movie that shows where and how electricity is made and much more.

Pages 22 - 23 Using electricity

Get hold of some old electrical devices such as old radios, torches or hairdryers and let the children unscrew and take them apart (under supervision) and follow and perhaps draw the parts inside, such as motors, or the electrical circuit that they find.

At http://www.digitalbrain.com/document.server/subjects/ks2sci/su4/mod1/pad_alarm.htm children can follow instructions to make a fun and simple pressure pad alarm.

Pages 24 - 25 Saving energy

There is some excellent information about various kinds of alternative energy, including wind, solar, biomass and geothermal, at http://www.energyquest.ca.gov/story/index.html

Children could work in teams to use the Internet to research and report on how energy could be used more efficiently around the school, including things like heat loss (insulation and draught-proofing) and lighting and heating in the school.

It's worth spending some time discussing the need to select information from the Internet carefully, rather than just taking notes from the first site they find. How do they think they can determine whether or not a source is likely to be reliable? They could present their report to a school council or head teacher and governing body.

There is a useful page about the meaning of energy efficiency labels at http://www.nationwide.co.uk/energy/energy_efficient_appliances.asp There is a concise guide to the benefits of energy saving at http://www.foe.co.uk//living/poundsavers/save_energy.html

Pages 26 - 27 Playing it safe

The electricity company npower has developed a simple game to deter primary aged children from playing around pylons and substations. The game, 'Safe Journey Home', is in the education section at http://www.npower.com/Education/Games.html

The children could devise their own safety games based on Snakes and Ladders. The danger squares (that send them back to the start or back a few squares) could have 'Danger of Death' signs on them and include warnings about what they did or might have done wrong, such as used a plug with a frayed cable.

If your school is located near to a power station you may be able to organise an educational visit. Many power stations have designated education departments and services.

To recap on the work in this book you could download the 'Night Night' worksheet in the 7-11 section at http://www.edfenergy.com/powerup

Index